PRESENTED TO:

Esmeralda Sánchez

FROM:

Chris Jordan

DATE:

June 1, 2020

THE Apostles' CODE

UNLOCKING THE POWER OF THE HOLY SPIRIT IN YOUR LIFE

O. S. Hawkins

COUNTRYMAN®

An Imprint of Thomas Nelson Publishers

THOMAS NELSON
Since 1798

Originally published as part of *The Passion Code*, © 2019, ISBN 978-1-4002-1150-0.

Published in Nashville, Tennessee, by Thomas Nelson. Thomas Nelson is a registered trademark of HarperCollins Christian Publishing, Inc.

Thomas Nelson titles may be purchased in bulk for educational, business, fund-raising, or sales promotional use. For information, please e-mail SpecialMarkets@ThomasNelson.com.

Unless otherwise noted, Scripture quotations are taken from the New King James Version®. © 1982 by Thomas Nelson. Used by permission. All rights reserved.

Scripture quotations marked NIV are taken from the Holy Bible, New International Version®, NIV®. Copyright © 1973, 1978, 1984, 2011 by Biblica, Inc.® Used by permission of Zondervan. All rights reserved worldwide. www.Zondervan.com. The "NIV" and "New International Version" are trademarks registered in the United States Patent and Trademark Office by Biblica, Inc.®

Scripture quotations marked AMP are from the Amplified® Bible. Copyright © 1954, 1958, 1962, 1964, 1965, 1987 by The Lockman Foundation. Used by permission. (www.Lockman.org)

Scripture quotations marked ESV are from the ESV® Bible (The Holy Bible, English Standard Version®). Copyright © 2001 by Crossway, a publishing ministry of Good News Publishers. Used by permission. All rights reserved.

Scripture quotations marked KJV are from the King James Version. Public domain.

All emphasis in scriptures is the author's.

ISBN 978-1-4002-2065-6

Printed in the United States of America

20 21 22 23 24 POL 10 9 8 7 6 5 4 3 2 1

INTRODUCTION

One of the saddest verses in the Bible is found in the aftermath of Jesus' arrest in Gethsemane's garden. Of the apostles, the Bible simply records, "Then they all forsook Him and fled" (Mark 14:50). They had been so bold and boastful of their commitment to Him just hours before. But when it came down to the crisis moment, they ran, they went AWOL, and they fled into the darkness when He needed them the most.

But what an amazing change came over them a few days later. Peter had denied He knew the Lord three times as he sat in the courtyard of Caiaphas's house, where Jesus was being imprisoned. But the transformation that soon would take place in his life is astounding. Hear him—after being beaten, imprisoned, and commanded to never speak the name of Jesus again—say in the face of his adversaries, "We cannot but speak the things which we have seen and heard" (Acts 4:20). What empowered Simon Peter and all the rest of the apostles to suddenly live with such boldness and meet their martyrs' deaths, answering with their lives the question asked by their

Lord, "Will you lay down your life for My sake?" (John 13:38). Pentecost had come. They had unlocked the code. The same Spirit that had raised Christ from the dead now lived in each of them, giving them supernatural power. And this same Spirit lives in you and me. This is the Apostles' Code: unlocking the power of the Holy Spirit in your life.

As you journey through these pages, you will meet the Holy Spirit afresh and anew. He, who has come to live in every believer, longs to fill us with His fullness and produce the fruit of His life through us. *The Apostles' Code* is written to move and motivate us to an intense desire to come to know the Holy Spirit and allow Him to fill us so we can be emboldened in Christ's service. It leads us on a forty-day journey with Jesus to discover the truth of Colossians 1:27, "To them God willed to make known what are the riches of the glory of this mystery among the Gentiles: which is *Christ in you*, the hope of glory."

Each daily reading embodies a Code Word that serves as a daily reminder unlocking the truth of the devotional thought that day. Write it down. Keep it with you. Think about it through your day as it stirs you to apply the truth to your daily life so that you, as James challenges, will become "doers of the word and not hearers only" (James 1:22, modified).

We have a God who still speaks to us personally by His Word and through His Spirit. Listen to His still, small voice leading you to yield to His Spirit so that you, like the apostles, might unlock the code: the power of the Holy Spirit in your own life.

The apostle Paul, when inquiring of those early believers in Ephesus about their knowledge of the Holy Spirit, was met with this reply: "We have not so much as heard whether there is a Holy Spirit" (Acts 19:2). Sadly, the same response could be heard from many believers today. The emphasis on who the Spirit is—and what He does—is lacking in much of the modern church. So, in these next few pages, let us set out to meet the Holy Spirit.

In short, the Holy Spirit is God Himself. An invisible yet inseparable person of the Trinity: the Father, the Son, and the Holy Spirit. Too often, He is the forgotten member of the Godhead. Much is made of the Father and the Son and not enough of the Spirit. The Holy Spirit is God coming to indwell us, never to leave us, and to empower us for Christian service. It is the Spirit who convicts us of our sin, draws us to Christ, seals our faith, and gives us power to live the Christian life.

If you have believed on Jesus Christ, then the Holy Spirit has come to take up residency in your life. He is alive *in you* right now!

Code Word: HOME

There is no place like home. And "home" for the Holy Spirit is in your heart. Today, when you come home and get comfortable, remember that your heart is where the Spirit of God lives and makes His home.

> To them God willed to make known what are the riches of the glory of this mystery among the Gentiles: which is Christ in you, the hope of glory.
>
> Colossians 1:27

....

Lord, thank You for the realization, right this very moment, that You—through Your precious Holy Spirit—are alive in me today. Lead me and use me for Christ's own glory. In Jesus' name, amen.

Promises made are valuable, but promises kept are invaluable. On the eve of the crucifixion, Jesus made an amazing promise to His disciples and to us: "I will pray the Father, and He will give you another Helper, that He may abide with you forever—the Spirit of truth" (John 14:16–17).

The key to understanding the true identity of the Holy Spirit is wrapped up within the word *another* in this promise. There are two Greek words translated into our English word *another*. One, *heteros*, means another, but of a different kind. We get our word *heterosexual* from this word. The other word, *allos*, means another of the exact same kind. For example, if I showed you a fountain pen and then showed you another pen—a cheap plastic pen—it would mean "another," but of a different kind. However, if I showed you a black Montblanc pen and then another one identical to it, then it would mean "another" of the exact same kind.

The latter is the word Jesus used in describing this Helper to come. In essence, Jesus was saying, "I am leaving, but I am coming back to abide in you forever. The Holy Spirit is *Me*!" He is the same make and the same model. Jesus kept His promise, and His Spirit comes to live in us, with the added promises to never leave us and to empower us to serve Him.

CODE WORD: PROMISE

Many of us are pretty good at making promises and then, for one reason or another, forgetting them or just not keeping them. But this never happens with Jesus. When you think about the promises you have made, let them remind you that Jesus always keeps His promises to you.

> For the promise is to you and to your children, and to all who are afar off, as many as the Lord our God will call.
>
> ACTS 2:39

Lord, thank You for the wonderful fact that You don't just make promises; You keep them. Great is Your faithfulness to me. In Jesus' name, amen.

One of the most liberating discoveries in the life of the believer is awakening to the importance of the personality and the deity of the Holy Spirit. If He is your constant companion, living in you, it stands to reason that you want to know Him in the intimacy of a close and abiding personal relationship.

Many are on a quest to "get more" of the Holy Spirit. But He is a Person, not some mystical force or substance. If we know Christ, we have all the Holy Spirit we will ever need. When we begin to think of Him in terms of some external force that might enable us or empower us with various kinds of supernatural abilities, then our quest will lead us on a journey to seek more of Him—and that is a dead-end road.

But when we think of Him as He really is, a Person, then our search will not be in trying to *get more of Him*; rather, we will be consumed with how we might *give Him more of us*. The Holy Spirit is a Person. He lives in you. His desire is to get more of you. And this happens when you surrender every area of your life to Him.

Code Word: ROOM

Like me, you have several rooms in your heart: a family room, a professional room, a social room, and so forth. Christ's desire is to be Lord over all the rooms in your life. Today, when you enter a room, let it remind you to search your own heart and give Him more of you!

> "He will give you . . . the Spirit of truth, whom the world cannot receive, because it neither sees Him nor knows Him; but you know Him, for He dwells with you and will be in you."
>
> JOHN 14:16–17

Lord, I have all of You I will ever need. The real question I must ask is, "Do You have all of me?" Search out my heart today and reveal those parts of me I have not yet given to You. In Jesus' name, amen.

E ach person of the Godhead plays a vital role in our salvation. The Father is the *source* of salvation. It all stems from Him. From the moment Adam and Eve ate of the forbidden fruit, and God slew an innocent animal to clothe them with its skins, His plan of salvation through blood atonement kicked into gear—culminating, ultimately, on a Roman cross outside the city gates of Jerusalem.

If the Father is the source, then the Lord Jesus is the *course* of our salvation. The road to an eternity with the Father must come through Him who said, "I am the way, the truth, and the life. No one comes to the Father except through Me" (John 14:6).

The Holy Spirit is the *force* behind it all. When giving final instructions to the disciples, Jesus said, "If I depart, I will send Him [the Holy Spirit] to you. And when He has come, He will convict the world of sin . . . [and] will guide you into all truth" (John 16:7–13).

The word *convict* means to bring to light, to expose, to show one's fault. The Holy Spirit flips the switch, turning on the light and exposing our sin. Being thus convicted of our own sin, the Holy Spirit then draws us close to Christ and performs the work of regeneration, for the Bible says we are born again "of the Spirit" (John 3:8).

CODE WORD: LIGHT SWITCH

Today, when you turn the light on in a darkened room, let it remind you of the convicting power of the Holy Spirit in your own life, exposing your sin before your eyes. Then confess it and forsake it!

> "He [the Holy Spirit] will glorify Me, for He will take of what is Mine and declare it to you."
>
> JOHN 16:14

Lord, You are my Convictor, Converter, Comforter, and Completer. Without You, I would be hopeless and helpless. Fill me with Your power today. In Jesus' name, amen.

There is something within most of us that loves to identify with certain brands. We wear clothing that proudly displays particular logos. Our key rings proclaim the logos of the cars we drive. And who of us with deep loyalty to our colleges or universities does not proudly proclaim it through all types of logos on bumper stickers, hats, and shirts?

Did you know that the Holy Spirit has some unique logos of His own that describe who He is and what He does? For example, fire is an emblem of the Holy Spirit. Fire speaks of the Spirit's consuming power in the life of the believer. John the Baptist told his followers in the Jordan valley that Jesus would "baptize [them] with the Holy Spirit and fire" (Matthew 3:11).

While the dove is perhaps the most prominent logo describing the Holy Spirit, another is wind. Wind speaks of the incredible depth of His mighty power to regenerate us. Jesus said, "The wind blows where it wishes, and you hear the sound of it, but cannot tell where it comes from and where it goes. So is everyone who is born of the Spirit" (John 3:8).

We may not be able to see the wind, but we can certainly see its power blowing the leaves in the trees. So it is with the Spirit. We may not be able to see Him, but we can certainly see the powerful effect of His presence all around us.

CODE WORD: BRAND

Today, if you pick up a writing pen with its logo or put on a shirt with its brand, let it be a reminder that the Holy Spirit desires to imprint your very soul with His own presence and identity for all the world to see.

> "By this all will know that you are My disciples, if you have love for one another."
>
> JOHN 13:35

Lord, in the midst of my identifying with so many good things, help me never to be ashamed of identifying with the greatest One of all—You! In Jesus' name, amen.

S ome believers today seem to be confusing two very
important words in our Christian vocabulary—
influence and *power*. We seem to pride ourselves on
influence, particularly when it comes to the arena of
politics. On every front, it seems we are seeking to
influence those in high places. We picket and protest,
pass resolutions and sign petitions. Some of us even
have access to the highest offices of the land to express
our grievances and our desires.

People in the early church faced plenty of challenges. Too often, they were trying to keep from being
burned at the stake or thrown to wild animals in one
of Caesar's venues. When you think about it, it makes
our problems—like fighting Washington to keep our
tax-exempt status intact—relatively mundane.

These early believers did not have enough *influence*
with the authorities to keep Peter out of prison (Acts
12), but they had something better. They had access
to the *power* of the Holy Spirit to pray him out . . . and
they used it!

The Holy Spirit living in you has far more power
to get things done than any influence you could ever
hope to wield.

Code Word: INFLUENCE

The Bible says each of us has been assigned an "area of influence" (2 Corinthians 10:13 ESV). In the midst of wielding your influence for good, don't forget that you have unlimited power—through the Holy Spirit who is dwelling in you right now!

> "You shall receive power when the Holy Spirit has come upon you."
>
> ACTS 1:8

. . . .

Lord, You said "all authority (all power)" is in You (Matthew 28:18 AMP). If all power, all authority is in You, and You have given Your authority to me (Luke 10:19), then Satan has none . . . except that which I yield to him and his deceit. Fill me with Your power today so there is no room for the evil one. In Jesus' name, amen.

After the resurrection, the band of believers huddled in the Upper Room in Jerusalem with explicit instructions from the Lord: "Wait for the Promise of the Father . . . 'you shall be baptized with the Holy Spirit'" (Acts 1:4–5).

Waiting is something many of us are not very good at. But waiting on the Lord is an essential element of Christian growth. Luke records Christ's final words to His followers immediately before "He was parted from them and carried up into heaven" (Luke 24:51). He said, "Behold I send the Promise of My Father upon you; but tarry in the city of Jerusalem until you are endued with power from on high" (v. 49).

When reading this in the original Greek text, we discover an amazing truth. The word *endued* is in the middle voice. That is to say, the subject is not acted on by another but acts on itself for its own benefit. What happened in the Upper Room before the Holy Spirit fell on the believers? Jesus' followers were getting themselves right with God and then getting right with each other. They were not passively sitting around, waiting. They were taking action on themselves. When we get right with God ourselves—and get right with others in the process—we, too, can expect God to manifest His awesome presence in our lives.

Code Word: WAIT

Today when you have to wait for a phone call, a table at a restaurant, or an appointment with your doctor, let it be a reminder of the importance of patience, of waiting for the promise of your Father.

> Wait on the Lord; be of good courage, and He shall strengthen your heart; wait, I say, on the Lord!
>
> Psalm 27:14

. . . .

Lord, help me see how moments of waiting are really a laboratory for learning the depth of Your rich truths. In Jesus' name, amen.

DAY 8

The streets of Jerusalem were jammed with the masses of Jews who had descended on the city for the celebration of Pentecost, fifty days after the Passover. Jesus had ascended to heaven and, obedient to His instructions, the disciples had gathered in the Upper Room. On the day of Pentecost, suddenly there came into their room the sound of a mighty rushing wind followed by the sight of tongues of fire resting on each one's head. Then the disciples began to speak in languages and dialects they did not know, and people heard these utterances—each in his own language. Then the Bible records, "They were all filled with the Holy Spirit" (Acts 2:4).

This was a onetime event when the Holy Spirit came to dwell in every believer with the promise never to leave. Pentecost can never be repeated any more than Bethlehem or Calvary. Bethlehem was a onetime event when God came to be *with* us. Calvary was a onetime event when we see God *for* us on the cross. In like manner, Pentecost was a onetime event when we see God *in* us.

It is Pentecost that marks the time and place—the when and the where—that God first sent His Holy Spirit to indwell all His believers, to empower them (and us) for service great and small . . . with the promise never to leave us.

Code Word: BIRTH

Pentecost marks the birth of the church, those of us throughout the generations whom God has called out of the world to become a part of His body. As you celebrate the birthdays of family and friends, let it be a reminder that you and I are a part of something supernatural, the church of the Lord Jesus Christ.

> Do not be drunk with wine, . . . but be filled with the Spirit.
>
> EPHESIANS 5:18

Lord, thank You for the realization that, by being born again, You dwell in me this very moment by Your Spirit. Fill me with Your presence and power. In Jesus' name, amen.

As I have read and reread the Bible in preparation for the writing of these devotions on the Holy Spirit, I have been captured by the word *suddenly*. We find it here again on the day of Pentecost when the believers "were all with one accord in one place. And *suddenly* there came a sound from heaven" (Acts 2:1–2). What took place that day was not the result of some process of growth and development. No one was taught how to do what happened. It was not manifested by merit. It was the work of God, and it came *suddenly*. The disciples were surprised by God!

One of the problems with our modern, sophisticated church is that some of us have lost our expectancy, the wonder of it all in the work of it all. Remember the shepherds of Bethlehem? They were out tending their sheep, just like any other night, when *suddenly* a great angelic choir announced the Savior's birth (Luke 2:13). Paul was en route to Damascus when *suddenly* he saw a light from heaven (Acts 9:3). He and Silas were once in jail when *suddenly* a violent earthquake opened the prison doors (Acts 16:26).

Oh, the possibilities for us if we would only live in the realm of expecting the unexpected—the *suddenly*—today!

CODE WORD: SUDDENLY

The next time you are surprised by something or someone, let it be a reminder that more often than not, when we least expect it, *suddenly* we can be surprised by God Himself.

> "When He, the Spirit of truth, has come, He will guide you into all truth."
>
> JOHN 16:13

Lord, help me live today expecting the unexpected, for You still have a way of suddenly making the impossible possible. In Jesus' name, amen.

O ne of the many miracles that took place on the day of Pentecost was the believers speaking in other "tongues." Perhaps no other subject in Scripture has been as misunderstood as this phenomenon that took place when the Holy Spirit fell on that little band of early believers.

The Bible records that they "began to speak with other tongues, as the Spirit gave them utterance" (Acts 2:4). The Greek word for "tongue" here is *glossa*. We get our English word *glossary* from this word. It is linguistic. These were known languages. They were languages foreign to the speaker—ones he or she had never heard—but that they were supernaturally empowered to speak. The actual miracle was in the hearing. The Bible says, "Everyone heard them speak in his own language" (v. 6). The word for "language" here is *dialectos*, from which we get our word *dialect*.

So what happened? People were there from all over the world for Pentecost, and God performed a miracle. Everyone heard the message of the gospel not only in his own language but in his own dialect. And the result? Three thousand Jews became followers of the Messiah on that very day and scattered back across the Mediterranean world to their homes sharing this good news.

Code Word: MIRACLE

Some miracles may come your way that are huge, with no explanation but the intervention of God on your behalf. But most of our miracles come day by day and often "suddenly," when we may least expect them.

> Though I speak with the tongues of men and of angels, but have not love, I have become sounding brass or a clanging cymbal.
>
> 1 Corinthians 13:1

....

Lord, the greatest miracle of all is the new birth . . . the way You met me where I was, forgave me of my sin, came into my life by Your Spirit, and live in me, now and forever. In Jesus' name, amen.

O n the day of Pentecost, not only were the believers "*all* with one accord in one place" (Acts 2:1), but they were "*all* filled with the Holy Spirit" (v. 4). Not some of them . . . all of them. They had been baptized into the body of Christ and sealed by the Holy Spirit, and now they were filled with all His fullness. While the baptism of the Holy Spirit is a once-and-for-all-time experience at conversion, the filling is to be repeated over and over in the Christian's experience. At conversion we have the Holy Spirit; when we are filled, He has us.

The Holy Spirit's work in our lives involves many factors. Among them is the baptism of the Holy Spirit found in 1 Corinthians 12:13: "For by one Spirit we were all baptized into one body." This brings about the indwelling of the Holy Spirit—"The Spirit of God dwells in you" (Romans 8:9). Then we are sealed with the Holy Spirit: "Having believed, you were sealed with the Holy Spirit" (Ephesians 1:13).

If you are a believer, God the Holy Spirit has come to live in you. And He is the guarantee, the seal, that secures your eternal destiny. No wonder Paul exclaimed, "Christ in you, the hope of glory" (Colossians 1:27).

Code Word: DOWN PAYMENT

A down payment is a good-faith gesture on our part that assures the ultimate completion of a transaction. The sealing of the Holy Spirit is God's down payment, the "guarantee of our inheritance until the redemption of the purchased possession, to the praise of His glory" (Ephesians 1:14).

> In Him you also trusted, after you heard the word of truth, the gospel of your salvation; in whom also, having believed, you were sealed with the Holy Spirit of promise.
>
> Ephesians 1:13

Lord, thank You for the realization that You are truly alive in me at this very moment and for the security of knowing I am "sealed" by Your Spirit, the guarantee of my inheritance in You. In Jesus' name, amen.

There is only one command in the Bible as it relates to the Holy Spirit. We are not commanded to be baptized in the Holy Spirit—if we have trusted in Christ, the Bible tells us we have already been baptized in Him. And we are not commanded to be sealed with the Holy Spirit, for this is God's own work in us. What we are commanded to do is found in Ephesians 5:18: "Do not be drunk with wine, in which is dissipation; but be filled with the Spirit."

Every verb has a number, tense, voice, and mood. When we parse this verb translated as "be filled," we discover that the number is plural. It is in the present tense, which indicates continuous action. The voice is passive, meaning that the subject doesn't act; it is acted on by another. And the mood is imperative. That means this is not optional; it is a direct command. Putting all this together means that this verse is more correctly translated as "All of us must always be being filled with the Holy Spirit."

God's desire is that instead of our trying to *get* more of Him, we might this very day *give* Him more of ourselves so that He might then fill us with His own Spirit and power.

Code Word: COMMAND

When you face issues in which you have no option, like paying your taxes or making a house payment, let it remind you that to be filled with all of God's presence and power is not an option but should be the daily, normal Christian life.

> For this reason I bow my knees to the Father of our Lord Jesus Christ, . . . that He would grant you, according to the riches of His glory, to . . . be filled with all the fullness of God.
>
> Ephesians 3:14–19

.....

Lord, strengthen me by Your mighty power through Your Holy Spirit today. In Jesus' name, amen.

I awoke early this morning with the incredible realization that the Holy Spirit was alive *in me*. Think
about that. And His desire is not to simply indwell us
today but to fill us each moment of every day with
His presence and power. Remember: God's only command regarding the Holy Spirit is this: "Be filled with
the Spirit" (Ephesians 5:18). And how can you be
filled, right this moment?

First, *confess* your sins to Him. Come clean. The
Spirit doesn't fill dirty vessels. The Bible promises, "If
we confess our sins, He is faithful and just to forgive
us our sins and to cleanse us from all unrighteous-
ness" (1 John 1:9).

Next, *crown* Jesus Lord of your life. Take yourself
off the throne of your heart and put Him there. "For
to this end Christ died and rose and lived again, that
He might be Lord of both the dead and the living"
(Romans 14:9).

Finally, *claim* this amazing truth by faith. Jesus
said, "Whatever things you ask when you pray, believe
that you receive them, and you will have them" (Mark
11:24).

What is more important: what God says or how
you feel? Don't equate warm, fuzzy feelings with being
filled by the Spirit—or the absence of those feelings

with an absence of the Spirit. Instead, know that you are filled according to your faith. Go ahead . . . *confess*, *crown*, and *claim* the Spirit's filling by faith.

CODE WORD: GLASS

When you fill your glass with water or iced tea, or when you fill your cup with coffee, let it remind you that God's will for you is to "be filled with the Spirit."

> And the disciples were filled with joy and with the Holy Spirit.
>
> ACTS 13:52

. . . .

Lord, I confess my sin to You, I crown You the Lord of my life, and I claim Your promises by faith. Fill me with joy and with the Holy Spirit. In Jesus' name, amen.

Anyone who has visited the Holy Land has likely been struck by the stark contrast of the two inland bodies of water in the state of Israel—the Sea of Galilee in the north and the Dead Sea in the south.

The Sea of Galilee is teeming with life, abundant with all types of thriving aquatic life. It is often crystal clear and a beautiful blue in color. The Jordan River's headwaters flow from a myriad of springs near Mount Hermon and journey south to where the river empties into the Sea of Galilee. From there, it finds its outlet at the southern end of the sea and continues its flow down the Jordan Valley until it empties into the Dead Sea.

The Dead Sea has earned its name for a reason. It is dead! No aquatic life whatsoever is found in its waters, and the sulfuric smell arising from it is nauseating.

What causes this difference between the two bodies of water? The Dead Sea has only an inlet. It takes in but does not give out. The Sea of Galilee, on the other hand, has both an inlet *and* an outlet. It not only receives; it gives away. So it is with the vibrant believer who not only receives God's fullness but also gives it away—and then, like the Sea of Galilee, is constantly being refilled with the Spirit.

CODE WORD: WATER

Whenever you see water today—whether it's in a sea, a lake, or a glass—let it remind you of these two very different bodies of water and of God's desire for you to be like the Sea of Galilee—receiving His fullness and giving it away.

"Freely you have received, freely give."

MATTHEW 10:8

. . . .

Lord, make me simply a channel of Your blessing today. Fill me so that Your power flows through me to touch and encourage someone who needs hope this very day. In Jesus' name, amen.

During my boyhood days, my family would make an annual summer trek from Texas to the mountains of Tennessee to visit my great-uncle and great-aunt. They owned a little one-room country store on the side of a mountain nine miles outside of Pikeville. I was a city boy and completely fascinated by life in the Tennessee hills without running water.

They had an old surface pump well outside the back door of their house. To use it, you would take a little water from a Mason jar and pour it into the pump to prime it. Then you would pump, pump, pump until the water started flowing. As long as you pumped, water would flow, but as soon as you stopped, so did the water.

There is another kind of well called an artesian well. It is dug deep until it hits an underground stream or river. You don't have to pump an artesian well. All you have to do is tap into it and the water flows and flows.

There are too many Christ followers like that old pump well. They are pretty shallow, and to get them to serve God, you have to prime the pump—and then pump, pump, pump. Then there are those who have tapped into the "river of life" and are being continuously filled with the Spirit. Their lives overflow with

His fullness. Some want to be served, while those filled with His fullness want to serve. Which one are you?

CODE WORD: FAUCET

When you turn the water faucet on to wash your face, brush your teeth, or get a drink, let it remind you to tap into the living water of the Spirit's own fullness.

> "Whoever drinks of the water that I shall give him will never thirst. But the water that I shall give him will become in him a fountain of water springing up into everlasting life."
>
> JOHN 4:14

....

Lord, I am thirsty for You. Spring up, O well, within my soul, and make me a blessing today. In Jesus' name, amen.

W here is the evidence that we are being filled with the Spirit of the living God? Some say the proof is found in certain gifts of the Spirit that we may be supernaturally enabled to perform. Yet we can read even the lengthiest passage about the gifts—1 Corinthians 12–14—and not find a syllable, much less a verse, about gifts being an indicator of being filled with the Spirit. The gifts of the Spirit are not a sign of spiritual maturity. In fact, Paul wrote to these same Corinthian believers, saying he could not speak to them "as to spiritual people but as to carnal, as to babes in Christ" (1 Corinthians 3:1).

The more we know our Bible, the more we understand the importance of context. Thus, the proof of God's fullness in a life is found in the very context of His command for us to "be filled with the Spirit" (Ephesians 5:18). There is no period at the end of verse 18, but rather a comma, with the next three verses offering the evidence of God's fullness in our lives.

First, there is an *inward* evidence. We will have a song in our hearts as we sing and make melody in our hearts to the Lord (v. 19). Then there is the *upward* evidence of an attitude of gratitude, "giving thanks always . . . to God" (v. 20). Finally, there is the *outward* evidence found in the fact that we are "submitting to one another" (v. 21). These—not supernatural gifts—are the proof of the Spirit-filled life.

Code Word: PROOF

Today, when you need to prove a point about something, remember that the proof of God's Spirit filling you is seen in the song in your heart, your attitude of thanksgiving, and your submissive spirit to others.

Let each esteem others better than himself.

PHILIPPIANS 2:3

Lord, if You humbled Yourself and became a servant, how much more do I need to see others today as better than myself? Fill me with Your fullness, and help me to serve others today. In Jesus' name, amen.

The *inward* evidence that you are being filled with God's Spirit is "singing and making melody in your heart to the Lord" (Ephesians 5:19). This is what separates Christianity from other religions. Buddhists may have impressive temples, but they have no song in their hearts. Hindus may have their mantras and chants but no melody in their hearts. Islam may pride itself on its morality and mosques, but Muslims have no song in their hearts. When we are filled with God's Spirit, the first evidence is an inward joy, a song in our hearts.

Those of us who cannot carry a tune are thankful the instrument of this song is our heart and not our vocal cords! We may not be able to make much melody with our voices, but we certainly can with our hearts.

Note it is "melody" and not rhythm or harmony that is the evidence of the Spirit. Whichever of these three—melody, rhythm, or harmony—is dominant in a piece of music generally points to its intended appeal. Rhythm appeals to the flesh. Harmony appeals to the realm of our emotions. But melody? It appeals to the Spirit, that part of us that will live as long as God lives, which is forever.

You will know you are being filled with God's

Spirit when you have a joyous song of melody welling up within you unto the Lord.

Code Word: SONG

Whenever you hear a song today—whether it's on the radio, in an elevator, or while you're waiting on hold—let it remind you of the inward evidence of God's Spirit working in your heart.

> Be filled with the Spirit, speaking to one another in psalms and hymns and spiritual songs, singing and making melody in your heart to the Lord.
>
> Ephesians 5:18–19

. . . .

Lord, You are the melody in my life. Without You, there is no lasting joy. My heart sings praises to You this day. In Jesus' name, amen.

There is also an *upward* evidence of the Spirit filling our lives: "giving thanks always for all things to God the Father in the name of our Lord Jesus Christ" (Ephesians 5:20). Note that our thanks is directed primarily "to God." When we realize that the Father is the source of everything and we allow His Spirit to fill us, our hearts will be full of thanksgiving "always" and "for all things."

I can hear those voices now: "But you don't know my problem." "But you don't know my husband." "But you don't know the situation I am in." You're right. I don't know. But God does, and this verse still says "always" and "for all things." Some of us think of giving thanks only when we get a blessing: we get a new job, we recover from an illness, or our wayward child comes home. But the evidence that God's own Spirit is filling us is that we give thanks "always for all things," even in the midst of our circumstances.

Remember Jonah? From inside the fish's belly, he said, "I will sacrifice to You with the voice of thanksgiving. . . . Salvation is of the LORD" (Jonah 2:9). And the very next verse says, "So the LORD spoke to the fish, and it vomited Jonah onto dry land." Thanksgiving will set you free. It is the upward evidence of the filling of the Spirit.

Code Word: FISH

The next time you order fish for lunch or dinner, or see a fish in an aquarium, let it remind you that your situation is no worse than Jonah's . . . and that giving thanks has a liberating effect.

> In everything give thanks; for this is the will of God in Christ Jesus for you.
>
> 1 Thessalonians 5:18

. . . .

Lord, thank You, not necessarily for everything, but in the midst of everything. As I am filled with Your Spirit, fill me also with an attitude of thanksgiving so that I might glorify You throughout this day and always. In Jesus' name, amen.

There is not only an inward and upward evidence to the filling of God's Spirit but an *outward* evidence as well. How will those who come into contact with us know that we are being controlled by God's Spirit? Paul framed it this way: by our "submitting to one another in the fear of God" (Ephesians 5:21). That is, we are to live our lives esteeming other people as better than ourselves and putting them before us. It's not the things we say or the terminology we use that lets people know we are filled with God's Spirit; rather, it is how we act in our personal relationships with others that reveals the Spirit at work within us.

Christ is our example. See Him in the Upper Room, washing the disciples' feet. The greatest among them became the servant of them all. In a matter of hours, His own feet would be nailed to a Roman cross, yet He knelt before each of the Twelve to wash their feet. And yes, even the feet of the one who would so soon betray Him.

It is important to remember that this submission to one another is to be done "in the fear of God." Living in the fear of God is not a fear that God might put His hand *on* us in retribution, but a fear that He might take His hand of blessing and anointing *away* from us. We should live each day being careful not to say or do anything that might cause God to remove His hand of blessing from our lives.

CODE WORD: SINK

When you stand at the sink to wash your hands or brush your teeth, let it be a reminder of Christ washing the disciples' feet and for you to take on the Spirit of Christ, which is that of a servant to all, "submitting to one another."

> "Whoever desires to become great among you, let him be your servant."
>
> MATTHEW 20:26

....

Lord, I am never more like You than when I am serving someone in a spirit of humility and submission. You must increase . . . I must decrease. Help me live out that truth today. In Jesus' name, amen.

Have you ever been thirsty? I mean really thirsty? You might be inclined to spend two dollars for a bottle of water on a really hot day, but how much would you give for it if you were lost in the desert and dying of thirst? Money wouldn't matter. A truly thirsty person would pay any price.

Jesus said, "If anyone thirsts, let him come to Me and drink. He who believes in Me, as the Scripture has said, out of his heart will flow rivers of living water" (John 7:37–38).

The reason many of us are not being filled today is because we are not really *spiritually* thirsty. Thirst is a craving. Some of us thirst for worldly pleasures: cars, houses, "stuff" in all its shapes and sizes. Jesus reminded the Samaritan woman—and us—that whoever drinks of the things the world has to offer "will thirst again, but whoever drinks of the water that I shall give him will never thirst" (John 4:13–14).

We all know whether we are thirsty—thirst is painful. But if we have to ask ourselves if we are thirsty spiritually, then the chances are pretty great that we aren't. Do not settle for seeking to satisfy your thirst with the temporary things of this world; instead, seek the living water only Jesus provides.

CODE WORD: THIRST

Each time you feel that tinge of thirst welling up inside you, remember how necessary it is to be thirsty for the deeper things of God.

> "Ho! Everyone who thirsts, come to the waters; and you who have no money, come, buy and eat."
>
> ISAIAH 55:1

....

Lord, as You invited, I come to You now and ask You to create a genuine thirst in me for the deeper things of Your Spirit. In Jesus' name, amen.

J esus' invitation to those of us who are thirsty is, "Let [them] come to Me and drink" (John 7:37). *Come* is one of the simplest words in our entire vocabulary. A little child understands the word and crawls to us to be picked up. Even our pets understand the word and rush to our sides. But in our more mature "wisdom," many of us hear Jesus' invitation to come to Him and seem to think He is saying, "Go." So we *go* and try to do more. We somehow think the busier we get with His work, the more we will please Him, when all along He is whispering, "Come to Me."

Come to Jesus, not to some new devotional program or some formula or even some spiritual gift. When we come to Jesus, we do with our hearts what little children learning to walk do with their feet. We simply come . . . to Jesus.

But that is not all we should do. It is not enough to thirst for Him or even to come to Him. His instructions are to "drink." Too many of us stop short. All the water in the world will not quench the thirst of a dying person unless he or she drinks! To drink of this water of life means to ask God to fill us with His Spirit.

Code Word: COME

Today, when your boss asks you to "come into the office," or your husband or wife says, "Come to the dinner table," let it remind you of Christ's invitation to come to Him at all times.

> "If anyone desires to come after Me, let him deny himself, and take up his cross daily, and follow Me."
>
> LUKE 9:23

Lord, I come to You. Take my will and my selfish pride and replace them with Your Spirit. I drink today of that fountain of life, and I hold fast to Your promise that I may never thirst again. In Jesus' name, amen.

In the midst of the Lord's invitation to us to come and drink, He inserted these words: "He who believes in Me, as the Scripture has said, out of his heart will flow rivers of living water" (John 7:38). God's blessings always turn on the hinge of faith. It is "he who believes in Me." Faith is the way we drink of this living water that satisfies our souls.

Jesus backed up this amazing promise by establishing a biblical basis for it from the Hebrew Bible: "as the Scripture has said." What Scripture? Jesus, no doubt, had in mind the words of the ancient prophet Isaiah: "The LORD will guide you continually . . . you shall be like a watered garden, and like a spring of water, whose waters do not fail" (Isaiah 58:11). Earlier the Lord had spoken to the Samaritan woman at the well, saying, "Whoever drinks of this water will thirst again, but whoever drinks of the water that I shall give him will never thirst. But the water that I shall give him will become in him a fountain of water springing up into everlasting life" (John 4:13–14).

The "living water" to which Jesus referred indicates that we are never to be stagnant; we are to be like a fountain or a river, always flowing to bless others.

Drinking of the water that Christ gives is less about *getting* a blessing and more about *being* a blessing.

Code Word: DRINK

Today, when you take a drink from your coffee cup, water bottle, or other drink, let each intake awaken in you the invitation from Christ to come to Him and drink. And out of your heart "will flow rivers of living water" that will bless others (John 7:38).

> But he who doubts is condemned if he eats, because he does not eat from faith; for whatever is not from faith is sin.
>
> ROMANS 14:23

Lord, You said that without faith it is impossible to please You. Not just hard to please You, but impossible! I do believe—and I pray that You would help me keep my faith firmly fixed on You. In Jesus' name, amen.

W hen we view the invitation to come to Jesus through the lens of the Greek text, it is passionately expressive: "If anyone thirsts, let him come to Me and drink" (John 7:37). The wording of the original text indicates this is a rather loud and deeply emotional outburst. Jesus was not speaking softly here. What amazes me is that we should even need this urging and that He should have to give it! Shouldn't it be the other way around? Shouldn't the tables be turned here? Shouldn't you and I be the ones pleading with Him to allow us to come? And yet it is Jesus who passionately pleads for us to come to Him!

I wonder who the thirsty ones are across the world right now. Some of us have tried so desperately to quench the thirst within our souls with the things this world offers—the new car, that certain someone, or any of a thousand other things. Yet it seems the more we have, the thirstier we become. Could it be that Jesus is opening your eyes to the reality that the something you think you need is really Someone?

CODE WORD: LOUD

Today, when you hear a loud voice or loud music, let it remind you that Jesus is standing before you, speaking with the most authoritative voice you have ever heard, looking at you with the most penetrating eyes you have ever seen, and pleading with you to come to Him.

> The Spirit and the bride say, "Come!" And let him who hears say, "Come!" And let him who thirsts come. Whoever desires, let him take the water of life freely.
>
> REVELATION 22:17

Lord, forgive me for thinking the things this world offers could ever truly satisfy. The something I have been searching for is really Someone . . . You. In Jesus' name, amen.

T he fruit of the Spirit is love, joy, peace, longsuffering, kindness, goodness, faithfulness, gentleness,
self-control" (Galatians 5:22–23). At first glance the
sentence structure appears to possess a grammatical
error—"The fruit of the Spirit *is* love, joy, peace," and
so on. But the apostle is absolutely correct. This nine-
fold fruit of the Spirit is the outward evidence of the
presence of the One living within us. The fruit of the
Spirit is beyond our natural ability to produce, for it
is inwrought and outworked by the Holy Spirit within
us. It is He who is the Author of these attributes and
the Source from which they flow. The fruit is *what we
are*, and it is wrought in us by *whose we are*—not by
anything *we do* in our own strength.

This fruit produced by the Spirit-controlled life
manifests itself in three areas. First, when God's Spirit
is ruling and reigning on the throne of your heart, it is
expressed in your *countenance*—that is, your personal
relationship with God, the expression of which is love,
joy, and peace. Second, it is visible in your *conduct*,
that is, in your relationship with others, the outward
expression of which is longsuffering, kindness, and
goodness. Finally, it is evidenced by your *character*—
who you are in your relationship with yourself—the

expression of which is faithfulness, gentleness, and self-control.

So, going forward, we must each ask ourselves this question: Is my life filled with the Spirit's fruit?

Code Word: GRAPE

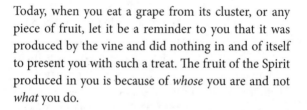

Today, when you eat a grape from its cluster, or any piece of fruit, let it be a reminder to you that it was produced by the vine and did nothing in and of itself to present you with such a treat. The fruit of the Spirit produced in you is because of *whose* you are and not *what* you do.

> "Therefore by their fruits you will know them."
>
> Matthew 7:20

....

Lord, it is not anything I do that will bring honor to Your great name, but rather it is what You do through me. The fruit of the Spirit is love, so let Your love be shown through me. In Jesus' name, amen.

"T he fruit of the Spirit is love, joy, peace . . ." (Galatians 5:22). The evidence of Spirit-filled living will not be in what we say or even in what we do. It will be written on our faces in our *countenance* of love, joy, and peace.

The first proof is found in *love*. The Greeks had three primary words that translate into our English vernacular as *love*. One is a fleshly, sensual, or passionate kind of love. Another is a fondness or affection, a kind of brotherly love. And then there is God's love, *agape*. This is a selfless love that seeks only the highest good for others—no matter what they may do to insult, injure, or humiliate us. *Agape* is the word Paul used here in Galatians 5:22. All the other manifestations of the fruit are simply different expressions of this agape love.

In addition to love, *joy* will also be evident on the face of a Spirit-controlled believer. This is not the sort of joy that comes from defeating an opponent or escaping some trouble. Instead, it is a joy that only God can give, a joy that persists and endures even when the shadows of life come our way.

And then there is *peace*, that blessed inner tranquility that the Spirit-filled believer is able to draw on when circumstances are anything but peaceful. It is the very peace Jesus promised when He said, "My peace I give to you; not as the world gives do I give to you" (John 14:27).

For the believer, love, joy, and peace join together to shine on our faces—and give glorious proof of the presence of the One who lives within us.

CODE WORD: COUNTENANCE

When you look in the mirror, what do you see in your face? Ask the Spirit to grow His fruit within you so that it shines on your countenance for all to see.

> The peace of God, which surpasses all understanding, will guard your hearts and minds through Christ Jesus.
>
> PHILIPPIANS 4:7

....

Lord, on my own, I can't love everyone, or be joyful in all things, or have peace in the midst of troubles. It is only through Your Spirit within me that I can be filled with Your love, Your joy, Your peace. Live through me to touch someone today. In Jesus' name, amen.

T he fruit of the Spirit is . . . longsuffering, kindness, goodness . . ." (Galatians 5:22). When we
live conscious of the Spirit's presence within us, we
will have not only a countenance that reflects His
presence but a conduct that reflects His character.
This is expressed in our ability to be longsuffering, to
offer kindness, and to exude goodness. And who of us
does not need a little more of these things?

To be *longsuffering* is to possess patience. The word
itself implies a refusal on our part to retaliate, even
when we have been wronged. It is an extension of
agape love—and love's greatest victory is often seen
not in what it does but in what it refuses to do.

Kindness is an attitude we can clearly see in the
life of Christ as He walked in this world. Simple but
intentional acts of kindness go a long way in enabling
others to see that Christ is alive in us. This kindness,
sometimes translated "gentleness," has nothing to
do with weakness. Rather, it is power on reserve and
definitive proof that God's Spirit is influencing our
lives.

And just as the Lord Jesus Himself "went about
doing good" (Acts 10:38), we Spirit-filled believers
will produce the fruit of goodness throughout our
lives in our relationships with others. Our world is

desperately looking for those who will offer patience, a little more kindness, and a lot more goodness. Won't you be one of them?

CODE WORD: STOPLIGHT

The next time you find yourself waiting at a stoplight, and the car in front of you doesn't go when the light changes to green, remember *Who* lives in you. Show some patience, a little kindness, and a lot more goodness to that driver—and to everyone in your day.

Rest in the LORD, and wait patiently for Him.

PSALM 37:7

Lord, I surrender anew to You so that when I come into contact with others today, they might see You—in me—demonstrated through longsuffering, kindness, and goodness. In Jesus' name, amen.

T he fruit of the Spirit is . . . faithfulness, gentleness, self-control" (Galatians 5:22–23). These three offer the third proof of a Spirit-filled life. In our relationship with God, we possess a countenance that is obvious: love, joy, and peace. In our relationship with others, we display a conduct that is characterized by longsuffering, kindness, and goodness. But what about the relationship we have with ourselves? Our character should be one defined by obedience, which reveals itself in faithfulness, gentleness, and self-control.

Faithfulness here does not mean our belief in God. Rather, it has more to do with the faithful discharge of the duties entrusted to us. A large part of having an obedient character is steadfast dependability and consistency, dedication and commitment. When we are being led by God's Spirit, we become known for our faithfulness to all things good.

Gentleness implies a kind of strength on a leash. The word Paul used here describes an animal that has been domesticated, that has come under the control of its master. The word picture is of a wild stallion that has been broken. Once untamed, kicking and bucking, it is now controlled by the slightest move of the reins, turning left or right, stopping or going at the wish of its master. Only Christ living in us can tame our sinful nature and bring it under such control that we express gentleness in all our relationships.

The last of the Spirit's fruit is *self-control*. This is the ability to master our own passions, to literally hold them in a firm hand. Self-control can never be fully realized on our own. It—like all the fruit—is produced only with the help of the Holy Spirit within us.

CODE WORD: PET

Today, when you give your pet instructions to come or to sit, and it responds in obedience, let it remind you that the Spirit living in you desires the same obedience from you.

If we live in the Spirit, let us also walk in the Spirit.

GALATIANS 5:25

Lord, true Christian character comes only from the power of Your Spirit. May my countenance, my conduct, and my character reveal Your presence in me to others today. In Jesus' name, amen.

Among my fondest childhood memories were the weekly Saturday morning football games on the old vacant lot. We began by choosing teams. There was one kid on my block that everyone wanted on their team. He was bigger and faster than the rest of us, and tougher to boot. When he was on your side, you knew you were on the winning team.

Are you aware that in the game of life, you have Someone very powerful on your side? That Someone is the Holy Spirit. The evening before the crucifixion, Jesus left His disciples—and us—with these words: "I will pray the Father, and He will give you another Helper, that He may abide with you forever" (John 14:16). And with the Spirit helping you, you can be sure that you are on the winning team.

The Greek word used here for *Helper* describes someone who is "called alongside" of you. This same word is translated "Advocate" in 1 John 2:1. The word picture is of you being charged with a crime and taken before the judge. You stand there all alone. And then a person approaches the bench and speaks on your behalf before the judge, brilliantly pleading your case. You have just such an Advocate on your side!

On that fateful evening Jesus was saying, "I am

leaving you, but the Holy Spirit is coming to be on your side and by your side. He will never leave you."

CODE WORD: LAWYER

The next time you see a lawyer's office or come in contact with a lawyer, let it be a reminder to you that God, in the person of the Holy Spirit, is always by your side and on your side.

> And if anyone sins, we have an Advocate with the Father, Jesus Christ the righteous.
>
> 1 JOHN 2:1

Lord, before anyone else, I choose You to be not just on my side but by my side . . . always and in all ways. In Jesus' name, amen.

A re you ready for an awesome thought to live with today? The Holy Spirit is alive and living *in you* right now! In fact, the Bible says, "Do you not know that your body is the temple of the Holy Spirit who is in you, whom you have from God, and you are not your own?" (1 Corinthians 6:19).

In the Old Testament, God had a temple for His people. There they would come to worship Him through the giving of their animal sacrifices. But in this new dispensation, God's temple is found in His people. You and me. We are His place of residence on this earth.

In the language of the New Testament, there are two Greek words we translate as *temple*. One describes the entire temple area and the Temple Mount, including the area where Jesus drove out the money changers (Mark 11:15). The other describes the inner sanctuary itself, the Holy of Holies. This is the holy place where only the high priest—and he only once a year—could enter and commune with the *shekinah* glory (the visible manifestation) of God Himself.

When Paul wrote of our body being the temple of the Holy Spirit, it was this latter word he used.

Think of it. You are God's Holy of Holies on earth. With such a Guest living in your heart, allow God to cleanse the temple of your heart today from anything and everything that might be unpleasing to Him.

Code Word: WORSHIP

Many of us are so body conscious. We trim and tone. Some of us even tuck! When thinking of your own body today, let it remind you that God is living *in you*, that you are His Holy of Holies—and take time to worship Him.

> For you were bought at a price; therefore glorify God in your body and in your spirit, which are God's.
>
> 1 Corinthians 6:20

Lord, to have paid such a high price for me, I must be of great value to You. Thank You for Your living presence in my life. Help me, each day, to more fully realize that You are truly alive in me. In Jesus' name, amen.

Have you ever had a confidential prayer partner? One you totally trusted and with whom you could confidentially share your deepest prayer needs? One who believed in you and with whom you agreed in prayer? Would you like to have a prayer partner like that? You already do! The Bible tells us, "The Spirit also helps in our weaknesses. For we do not know what we should pray for as we ought, but the Spirit Himself makes intercession for us. . . . He makes intercession for the saints according to the will of God" (Romans 8:26–27).

I don't know about you, but I often need help in prayer. I don't always know how I should pray about a matter. But the Holy Spirit in me does, and He always prays "according to the will of God." Yes, the Spirit can help you and me in our prayer lives. The word Paul used to describe how the Spirit helps us means literally to "lend a helping hand." The word picture is of two people carrying a log, one on either end, each dependent on the other to hold up his end. The same Greek word appears in Luke 10:40, when Martha appeals to Jesus to get her sister, Mary, to help her in the kitchen with the preparation of dinner. In the same personal and practical way, we need the Holy

Spirit to lend us a helping hand with our prayers—help we won't find in any earthly plan or program.

There is a powerful synergy at play when we recognize we have a personal prayer partner in the Holy Spirit—One who is not just by our side and on our side, but alive inside us.

CODE WORD: DINNER

The next time you prepare dinner, set the table, or sit down to dinner, remember Martha—and the way she needed Mary's help in the kitchen is the same way you need the Holy Spirit's help in your prayer life.

> [One could] chase a thousand, and two put ten thousand to flight.
>
> DEUTERONOMY 32:30

Lord, help me to know how to pray and what to pray and for whom to pray. I wait before You to listen to Your still, small voice. In Jesus' name, amen.

W e have a prayer partner, the Holy Spirit, who helps us in our "weaknesses" (Romans 8:26). And if you are like me, you are weak at times and need help with your prayer life. This should not come as a surprise. Do you remember the words of our Lord to His disciples in Gethsemane's prayer garden? "Could you not watch one hour?" (Mark 14:37). Jesus knew our weakness, so He sent us a prayer partner, the Holy Spirit, to help us.

The truth is we are no different from those men and women we read about in the New Testament. We "do not know what we should pray for as we ought" (Romans 8:26). Even the great apostle Paul unsuccessfully prayed three times regarding what he called a "thorn in the flesh" (2 Corinthians 12:7). And then he heard from his prayer partner. The Holy Spirit whispered, "My grace is sufficient for you, for My strength is made perfect in weakness" (v. 9).

The Holy Spirit lives in us to help us in our prayers, for we are all weak. We so often confuse our needs with our wants and do not know what is in our best interest. And there are times when we simply "do not know what we should pray." The something or someone we think we want is often not the something or someone we really need. But the Spirit knows exactly what we truly need—and He lovingly intercedes on our behalf with the Father.

Code Word: WANT

Today, when you see something you want, stop and ask yourself if it is something you really need. Many people run into heartaches in life because they get what they wanted, only to find out it was not what they really needed.

> And lest I should be exalted above measure by the abundance of the revelations, a thorn in the flesh was given to me. . . . I pleaded with the Lord three times that it might depart from me. And He said to me, "My grace is sufficient for you, for My strength is made perfect in weakness."
>
> 2 Corinthians 12:7–9

Lord, help me filter all my wants through the lens of what I truly need—those things that are for Your glory and my own good. In Jesus' name, amen.

We often speak of Paul writing the book of Romans, or John writing the Revelation, or Luke writing Acts. But the truth is, they, along with all the other Bible writers, were simply God's instruments through whom He gave us His Word. The Bible declares that "*all* Scripture is *given* by inspiration of God" (2 Timothy 3:16).

Inspiration means the words are God's words, but He chose to deliver them through human channels. Peter shared the key that unlocks this mystery when he wrote, "Holy men of God spoke as they were moved by the Holy Spirit" (2 Peter 1:21). The Greek word translated "moved" is also found in the account of Paul's shipwreck, when he found himself in the midst of a violent storm accompanied by raging winds. Paul tells us that the sailors on board "could not head into the wind, we let her drive" (Acts 27:15).

Just as the sailors were active on board the ship, even though they had no control over where it went, so were the Bible writers. Though their personalities and styles are apparent, the writings were not their own. They were "moved" by the Holy Spirit to write what they wrote. The Bible you own was not given to you by those writers but by God Himself through the inspiration of the Holy Spirit. No wonder we call it the Word of God!

Code Word: BOAT

When you see a boat or an image of one, let it always remind you that "all scripture is given by inspiration of God." While the Bible writers were active in their writing, the words they wrote down were beyond their control. The Bible is God's inspired Word.

> Then the LORD put forth His hand and touched my mouth, and the LORD said to me: "Behold, I have put My words in your mouth."
>
> JEREMIAH 1:9

....

Lord, Your Word is a lamp unto my feet today and a light unto my path. Thank You for sending this love letter to me personally. In Jesus' name, amen.

W e make much of the fact that Jesus forgives our sins. But did you know there is one sin that has no forgiveness? It is not murder or adultery or any of those other more blatant transgressions we are so skilled at pointing out in others. The Bible says, "Therefore I say to you, every sin and blasphemy will be forgiven men, but the blasphemy against the Spirit will not be forgiven men" (Matthew 12:31).

This unpardonable sin is not an act. It is not murder or adultery, and it is surely not something you might ignorantly say with your lips. The unpardonable sin is an attitude. Among the more memorable things Jesus said on His last evening on earth was, "When He, the Spirit of truth, has come, He will guide you into all truth" (John 16:13). To blaspheme the Holy Spirit is to reject His witness to your heart about who Jesus Christ really is—the Son of God. And if anyone reaches that point, his sin is unpardonable, and he is without hope.

This sin is not against the Father. Nor is it against the Son. It is against the Holy Spirit. It is not unpardonable because the Spirit is greater than the Father or the Son . . . but because His efforts come later! The Holy Spirit is God's final attempt to reach your soul with the message of salvation. The Holy Spirit is God going as far as He can to save you without making you a puppet and overruling your will.

Code Word: CALLOUS

Look at that callus on your hand or foot. You can stick a pin in it and not feel it. A callus is to your hand what a calloused attitude is to your heart: hardened and unfeeling. We get our word *callous* from the same Greek word Paul used to describe those who become "past feeling" (Ephesians 4:19). It is not that God no longer calls us to Him but that we can no longer hear Him. So when you see that callus, remind yourself not to let your heart get calloused.

> Today, if you will hear His voice, do not harden your hearts.
>
> Hebrews 3:15

Lord, my heart is open to hear Your voice right now. Speak, Lord—I wait before Your throne; Your promises I believe. And like Jacob of old, I will not let You go until Your blessing I receive. In Jesus' name, amen.

Did you know that when you become a believer, God stamps you with His seal of approval? The Bible says that when you put your trust in Christ, "you were sealed with the Holy Spirit" (Ephesians 1:13).

In the ancient world a seal was used to authenticate a document. A letter would be secured with hot wax and then *sealed* with the imprint of a signet ring to show it was real. The Holy Spirit is our seal to prove we are saved and secure: "The Spirit Himself bears witness with our spirit that we are children of God" (Romans 8:16).

A seal also shows ownership. Cowboys brand their cattle with hot irons to forever show others who the owner is. God seals us with His Spirit to let the world know we are His prized possessions and that we belong to Him, having been purchased at a great price.

The seal of the Holy Spirit also shows that we are secure—no one can snatch us away from God (John 10:28). The Roman soldiers sealed the tomb of Christ to secure His body and to prevent anyone from stealing it or tampering with it. Little did they know that their efforts to seal the *outside* of the tomb were useless against the power of the Lord *inside* the tomb! The same power that raised Jesus from the grave secures you in Him.

God has placed His own seal on you. It proves you are authentic, that you belong to Him, and that He will keep you secure forever.

Code Word: NOTARY

The next time you see a notary seal proving a document's authenticity, let it be a reminder of the seal stamped on your own heart—the seal of the Holy Spirit.

> Do not grieve the Holy Spirit of God, by whom you were sealed for the day of redemption.
>
> Ephesians 4:30

. . . .

Lord, may I live this day in such a way that it will be obvious to others that I bear Your brand, Your mark, Your seal on my heart. I want all the world to know that I belong to You. In Jesus' name, amen.

We are all familiar with bank deposits. The problem many of us face is making sure the deposits are enough to cover the expenses! Did you know that God has placed a deposit in you? The Bible says that God gives us the Holy Spirit, "who is a deposit guaranteeing our inheritance until the redemption of those who are God's possession" (Ephesians 1:14 NIV).

This deposit, or guarantee, is a promise of something more to come. Think of it this way: when you purchase a home, you put down a deposit—a down payment—showing good faith that you will complete the transaction. The Holy Spirit is God's down payment, placed in your life and stating to all that your final purchase is guaranteed.

The Holy Spirit in us assures us that the One who bought us with the price of His own blood is coming back. He is our "guarantee . . . *until* the redemption of the purchased possession" (Ephesians 1:14). If you put a $10,000 deposit down on a home, you are going to show up for the closing! Jesus paid a far greater price for you. And the Holy Spirit is His guarantee that He is going to return for you. Jesus will show up to close the deal.

CODE WORD: PAYCHECK

When you deposit your paycheck, let it remind you of the deposit God has placed in your heart . . . and the promise that eternal life is guaranteed to all those who believe and follow Him.

> In Him we have redemption through His blood, the forgiveness of sins, according to the riches of His grace.
>
> EPHESIANS 1:7

. . . .

Lord, the joy of knowing You and loving You in the here and now is but a foretaste of what it will be in the then and there. I look forward to the day when You "close the deal" on the deposit You made in me. In Jesus' name, amen.

I wasn't a follower of Christ very long before a well-meaning friend asked me if I had been baptized in the Holy Spirit. Some believe this is a second work of grace after conversion, leading to a deeper life. Others attest to it being the second half of the first work of grace. But the biblical reality is that this baptism is not a baptism *of* the Holy Spirit but a baptism *by* the Holy Spirit into the body of Christ. The Bible says, "For by one Spirit we were all baptized into one body" (1 Corinthians 12:13).

The Holy Spirit is the baptizer who, upon our conversion, immerses us into the body of Christ. For thirty-three years the world looked on the physical body of Christ. With His feet He walked among us, sometimes among great crowds and sometimes in the solitude of a single person. From His lips came the tenderest, most penetrating words ever spoken. Through His piercing eyes He looked straight into His people's hearts. Through His ears He listened intently to pleas for mercy. Through His hands He touched the points of greatest need.

Today, you and I are the visible "body of Christ" being watched by a needy world so desperately in need of His touch. We each have a special place in His body—the church. And just as with our own bodies, when one part of the body suffers, it affects the entire body. You are vital to God, and His body will never be complete without you serving in the part to which you are assigned. There is something for you to do in Christ's body—something that no one else can do like you. Are you doing your part?

CODE WORD: DEPENDENT

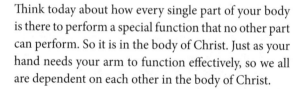

Think today about how every single part of your body is there to perform a special function that no other part can perform. So it is in the body of Christ. Just as your hand needs your arm to function effectively, so we all are dependent on each other in the body of Christ.

> For as many of you as were baptized into Christ have put on Christ.
>
> GALATIANS 3:27

Lord, what a privilege to be part of Your body, the church. Help me live in harmony with the other members so we might present the world with a beautiful picture of You. In Jesus' name, amen.

The church, born on the day of Pentecost, is supernatural in its origin. It is also supernatural in its operation. "When He ascended on high, He . . . gave gifts to men" (Ephesians 4:8). Every believer (that includes you) has been given a spiritual gift "for the equipping of the saints for the work of ministry, for the edifying of the body of Christ" (v. 12). These gifts are given by God; they are not sought, caught, bought, or taught. In Romans 12, we find there are gifts of mercy, service, teaching, exhortation, giving, leadership, and the like. In 1 Corinthians 12, there are gifts of knowledge, faith, and various other supernatural strengths.

These sovereignly bestowed gifts are not rewards, nor are they natural abilities. They are supernatural gifts, given to every believer. No one has every gift, and no one gift is given to every believer. The gifts are distributed in God's perfect wisdom—and that is good! Because who of us would have gifted some rough, raw, callus-handed fishermen with the ability to preach, teach, heal, and bring thousands upon thousands to the foot of the cross in one generation?

You will learn to recognize your own gift—it's the thing you love to do, the thing that energizes you. For example, if mercy is your gift, you will find your greatest joy in reaching out to those in need. Your gift will also be publicly recognized. The body of Christ will use it—and God will be glorified by it.

CODE WORD: USE

The next time you use a gift someone has given you, remember the special and supernatural gift God has given you. Use it to build up the body of Christ all around you.

> To each one of us grace was given according to the measure of Christ's gift.
>
> EPHESIANS 4:7

....

Lord, all the natural ability in the world that I may possess will never compare to the power of the spiritual gift You have entrusted to me. Lead me to use it well. In Jesus' name, amen.

When you pray, are you aware that the entire Godhead—the Father, the Son, and the Holy Spirit—is at work?

The *source* of our prayer is the Father. All true prayer begins when we claim our relationship with Him: *our Father*. And the only way we can truly call Him Father is to be born again into His forever family. The Bible says, "As many as received Him, to them He gave the right to become children of God, to those who believe in His name" (John 1:12). We are all God's creation, but we are not God's children until we put our faith and trust in Him alone.

The *course* of our prayer is the Son. There is no access to the Father except through Jesus the Son, as the Bible plainly teaches, "There is one God and one Mediator between God and men, the Man Christ Jesus" (1 Timothy 2:5). Access to the Father in prayer is not through a priest or a church, or through anything or anyone apart from Jesus Christ.

The *force* of our prayer is the Spirit. "The Spirit also helps in our weaknesses. For we do not know what we should pray for as we ought, but the Spirit Himself makes intercession for us . . . according to the will of God" (Romans 8:26–27). He is the force behind our prayers because He always prays according to God's will.

You may recite prayers and repeat phrases without the Holy Spirit. But you can never enter the Father's throne room of prayer unless you come through Jesus by the power of the Holy Spirit.

Code Word: TRAFFIC

The next time you use a GPS to get you where you need to go, let it remind you that the only way to reach the Father in prayer is through His Son and by His Spirit.

> Now this is the confidence that we have in Him, that if we ask anything according to His will, He hears us. And if we know that He hears us, . . . we know that we have the petitions that we have asked of Him.
>
> 1 John 5:14–15

Father, I come into Your presence only through the shed blood of Jesus Christ. Lead me to Your will for my life today through Your Word and by Your Spirit. In Jesus' name, amen.

Have you awakened to the reality that Christ is really alive *in you* in the person of His Holy Spirit at this very moment? The night before the crucifixion, Jesus said, "At that day you will know that I am in My Father, and you in Me, and I in you" (John 14:20). Today, fix your thoughts not on who you are, or what you are, or why you are, but on *where* you are.

Jesus revealed that He is positioned in the Father. Then, in the next breath, He said, "You [are] in Me"! No matter what may come your way today, you are in a good place. You are in Christ, and Christ is in the Father. Nothing can get to you that does not first have to pass through God the Father and God the Son to reach you. And if it penetrates that shield and gets that far, you can rest in the fact that there is a purpose for it in your life.

But that is not all. Jesus continued, "And I [am] in you." Can you see it? Christ is taking care of the outside of you (you are in Him), and He is also taking care of the inside of you (He is in you). What better place to live and have your being today!

CODE WORD: INSULATION

When you walk in your house and feel the warmth on a cold day or the cool on a hot day, that comfort is due, in large part, to the insulation you can't even see. Let that insulation remind you that, although you are not isolated from the world, you are insulated. You are in Christ, and He is in the Father—and in you.

> "Nevertheless I tell you the truth. It is to your advantage that I go away; for if I do not go away, the Helper will not come to you; but if I depart, I will send Him to you."
>
> JOHN 16:7

Lord, it is not who or what I am that matters to You . . . it is where I am: in You! In Jesus' name, amen.

The Bible is filled with invitations to come to God. Elijah of old challenged his hearers, pleading, "How long will you falter between two opinions? If the Lord is God, follow Him; but if Baal, follow him" (1 Kings 18:21). Joshua called the people of Israel to "choose for yourselves this day whom you will serve" (Joshua 24:15). Throughout the Old and New Testaments, bold voices continued to call men and women to faith in God.

The last invitation in the Bible is in Revelation 22:17: "The Spirit and the bride say, 'Come!' And let him who thirsts come. Whoever desires, let him take the water of life freely." Here we see not one, but two calls. There is an *outward* call: "The bride say[s] 'come!'" The bride of Christ is the church. This outward call is given by the church in a myriad of ways through sermon and service. There is also an *inward* call: "The Spirit says come." This is the call of God Himself, knocking at the door of our hearts. We find this inward call in the experience of Lydia in the Bible when we read, "The Lord opened her heart to heed the things spoken by Paul" (Acts 16:14). Paul had given the outward call, but it was the Holy Spirit who issued the inward call to her heart, bringing about a transformation of life.

How can two people read a devotional book such as this, and one person experiences no real urging or need to come to Christ, while another person is drawn by supernatural power to a faith in Christ? One person may hear only the outward call, but the other also hears the inward call of the Spirit saying, "Come to Jesus."

"Today, if you will hear His voice, do not harden your [heart]" (Hebrews 3:15)—come to Jesus.

Code Word: RSVP

The next time you receive an invitation and are asked to RSVP, let it remind you of Jesus' invitation. He is saying to you, "Come," and the Spirit—in His still, small voice—is saying the same thing. Won't you come?

> For as many as are led by the Spirit of God, these are sons of God.
>
> Romans 8:14

Lord, thank You for taking the initiative, for inviting me to come to You . . . before I ever thought of coming to You on my own. In Jesus' name, amen.

EPILOGUE

I t may be that you have no problem believing that God is with us; that He came to Bethlehem and clothed Himself in human flesh and walked among us. You may even believe the message of the cross: that Christ died for our sins, that He went to Calvary to die the death we deserved and to take our sin in His own body on the cross . . . God for us. But the question of eternity is this: Is God *in you*? Have you come to the place in your life—believing He came to be with us and died for us—where you have asked Him to forgive you of your sin and have transferred your faith and trust from your own human efforts to Him alone for eternal salvation?

It is impossible that the God of the universe, in the person of the Holy Spirit, has come to live *in you* and you do not know it. The Bible says the salvation experience is like going from death unto life (1 John 3:14), from darkness into light (1 Peter 2:9). Would it be possible to go from death unto life and not know it? Would it be possible to go from darkness into light and not know it? If there is the slightest doubt in your heart about whether Christ lives in you, you can settle it right now.

All other world religions are taken up with man trying to get to God through human effort, good works, almsgiving, and so on. What makes Christianity different from all others is that it is not the story of man trying to get to God, but the story of God coming to man. God with us. God for us. God in us.

Jesus said, "Behold, I stand at the door and knock. If anyone hears My voice and opens the door, I will come in to him" (Revelation 3:20). Picture, for just a moment, an imaginary door on your heart. Jesus, who came to be with us and died for us, is knocking on that door . . . right now. If you would like to receive God's free offer of eternal life, you can respond now by opening the door and inviting Him into your life. And when you do, you can stand on His promise, "Whoever calls on the name of the LORD shall be saved" (Romans 10:13).

If this is the desire of your heart, you can pray the following prayer. Go ahead, in your heart pray this:

Dear Lord Jesus,

I know I have sinned. I know I do not deserve eternal life. Please forgive my sin. Thank You for coming to be with me by taking my sin in Your own body and dying on the cross for me. My desire is for You to live in me now and forever. So I invite You now to be the Lord and King of my life. I turn to You, accepting Your gracious gifts of forgiveness of sin and eternal life. Thank You, Lord, for coming into my life as my Savior and my Lord. In Jesus' name I pray, amen.

A simple prayer can never save you, but Jesus can—and He will—if this prayer expresses the intense desire of your heart. You can now claim the promise Jesus left to all of us who would follow after Him: "Most assuredly . . . he who believes in Me has everlasting life" (John 6:47).

Now you have unlocked the Apostles' Code and are ready to live the great adventure for which you were created in the first place—to know Christ and to walk with Him daily, being filled with His Spirit. And as you do, His Spirit now abiding *in you* will be at work to continue transforming you, making you more like Jesus in character and integrity.

One final thought. If it is great to get a blessing, it is much greater to be a blessing. Someone you know needs to know Him. If *The Apostles' Code* or any of the other books in the Code series have been a blessing to you, become Christ's hand extended by giving a copy to a family member or friend.

MISSION:DIGNITY

All the author's royalties and any additional proceeds from the Code series (including *The Apostles' Code*) go to the support of Mission:Dignity, a ministry that enables thousands of retired ministers (and in most cases their widows) who are living near the poverty level to live out their days with dignity and security. Many of them spent their ministries in small churches that were unable to provide adequately for their retirement. They also lived in church-owned parsonages and had to vacate them upon their vocational retirement as well. Mission:Dignity tangibly shows these good and godly servants they are not forgotten and will be cared for in their declining years.

All the expenses for this ministry are paid for out of an endowment that has already been raised. Consequently, anyone who gives to Mission:Dignity can be assured that every cent of their gift goes straight to one of these precious saints in need.

Find out more by visiting missiondignity.org and clicking on the Mission:Dignity icon, or call toll-free at 877-984-8433.

ABOUT THE AUTHOR

For more than twenty-five years, O. S. Hawkins served pastorates including the First Baptist Church in Fort Lauderdale, Florida, and the First Baptist Church in Dallas, Texas. A native of Fort Worth, he has three earned degrees (BBA, MDiv, and DMin) as well as several honorary degrees. He is president of GuideStone Financial Resources, which serves 250,000 pastors, church staff members, missionaries, doctors, nurses, university professors, and other workers in various Christian organizations with their retirement and benefit service needs. He is the author of more than forty books, including the bestselling *The Joshua Code*, *The Jesus Code*, and *The James Code*, and preaches regularly at conferences, universities, business groups, and churches across the nation. He and his wife, Susie, have two married daughters and six grandchildren.

Follow O. S. Hawkins on Twitter @oshawkins.
Visit www.oshawkins.com for free resources.

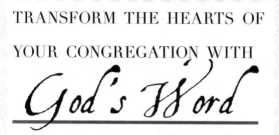

UNLOCK THE BLESSINGS

OF

God's Word

Do you long to experience the joy and peace only found in knowing and loving our Lord? *The Passion Code* leads you to grow closer to God and to discover that the more you know Him, the more you want to do His will.

ISBN: 978-1-4002-1150-0

One hundred percent of the author's royalties and proceeds go to support Mission:Dignity—a ministry providing support for impoverished retired pastors and missionaries.

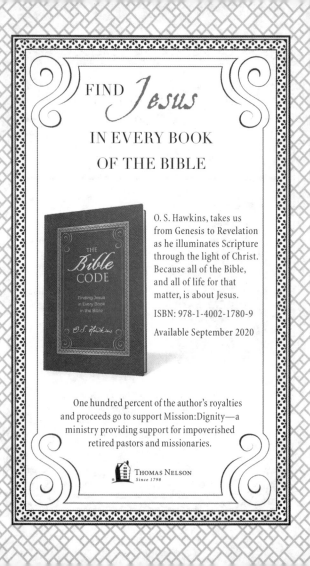